# INDEPENDENT AND UNOFFICIAL

# ROBLOX MASTER GAMER'S GUIDE

**The ultimate guide to finding, making and beating the best ROBLOX games!**

**THIS IS A CARLTON BOOK**

Published in 2018 by Carlton Books Limited, an imprint of the Carlton Publishing Group, 20 Mortimer Street, London W1T 3JW

Text and design © Carlton Books Limited 2018

This book is not endorsed by Roblox Corporation.
All information correct as of July 2018.

All screenshots and images of Roblox gameplay © Roblox Corporation.

A catalogue record for this book is available from the British Library.

ISBN: 978 1 78739 212 0

Printed in China

10 9 8 7 6 5 4 3

Designed and packaged by: Dynamo Limited
Writer: Kevin Pettman

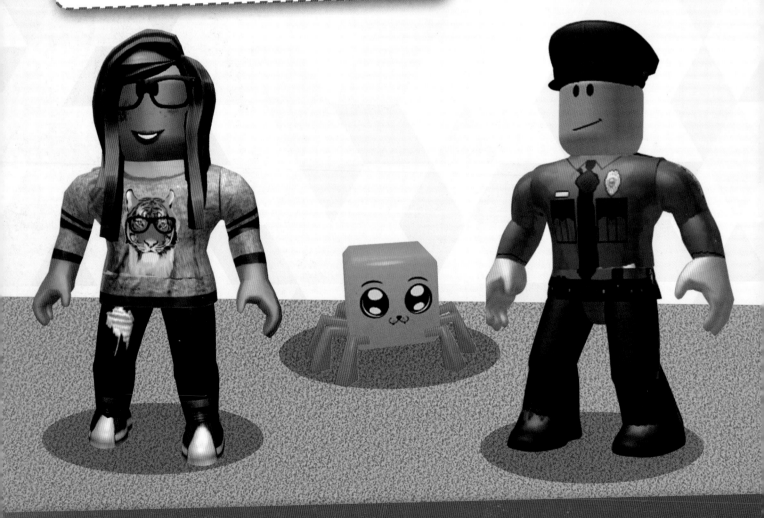

# ROBLOX MASTER GAMER'S GUIDE

CARLTON BOOKS

# CONTENTS

LOADS OF COOL STUFF INSIDE

**ROBLOX** is one of the biggest computer games in the history of the Universe! Well, except that it's not in the Universe – it's a spectacular virtual world created by gamers and building fans just like you.

 AWESOME!

With millions of fun and free user-generated games, like **Jailbreak** and **Work at a Pizza Place**, you'll enjoy hours of action and laughs exploring the ROBLOX world. This epic book is your ultimate game guide and is full of tips, info, facts, secrets and cool pictures. Join the block-tastic and brick-illiant fun now!

| PAGE | CONTENT |
|---|---|

## STAYING SAFE ONLINE

ROBLOX is a free online game that lets players choose from a huge selection of activity games. Users set up their character profile and control that character in games. ROBLOX users can 'chat' through the text feature, which can be restricted to friend-only chat or switched off completely. Chat has a filter and moderation system and users aged 12 and under can only communicate with gamers they accept as friends. For more info about staying safe in ROBLOX, see pages 18-19.

SERIOUS BIT!

# A NEWBIE'S* QUICK GUIDE

* A 'NEWBIE' IS A PLAYER WHO'S NEW TO THE GAME!

This speedy summary will rocket you through ROBLOX and reveal the big things you need to know!

ROBLOX can be played on PC, Mac, Xbox One, tablet and smartphone with internet access. It attracts over **23 MILLION NEW PLAYERS** each month, and was first released in 2006.

THERE ARE MILLIONS OF GAMES LIKE THIS!

**ROBLOX** provides the building and creating tools for its users to design and make their very own games. Each one of the millions of games have been created by people just like you!

## ROBLOX FACT!

ROBLOX pays some of the elite game creators over $250,000 a year, and more than two million users have built games.

The **ROBLOX STUDIO** is your virtual toolbox where you can learn how to make games and playable environments. The cool **ROBLOX Creator Challenge** helps to get you creating and coding, too.

YOU CAN CREATE ALL THIS!

Games can be about completing missions, superheroes, battle royales, vehicle simulators, roleplaying, building, mining – anything your imagination can conjure up!

ROBLOX is free to download and the vast majority of games are free to play. To play some games you need to pay with **Robux**, which is the in-game currency.

Players get Robux by using real-world money. With Robux you can also upgrade your **player avatar's** (character's) appearance.

R$

COOL OUTFIT!

Players can **chat** and communicate to others in ROBLOX through the chat system. **Friends** can connect and play games together, and even record the games they have.

# YOUR AWESOME AVATAR!

Give yourself a cool character look by creating an epic game avatar!

Once you've downloaded ROBLOX and set up your account, the first thing you should do is sort out your appearance. Select **Avatar** on the screen and you'll see your default setting.

YOU

YOUR FAVE SHIRT!

YOUR BFF

TRY A NEW HAIRSTYLE!

BUILD A PET!

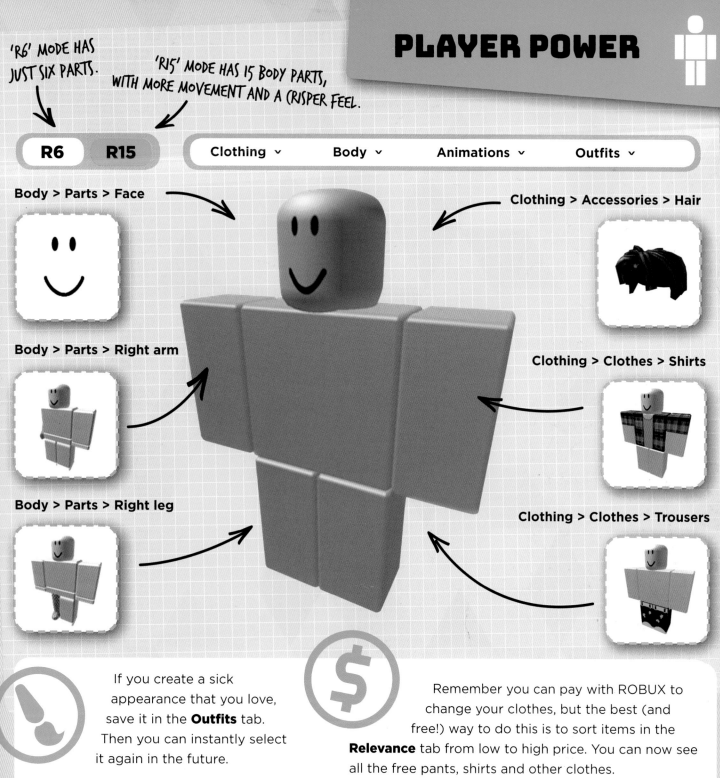

'R6' MODE HAS JUST SIX PARTS.

'R15' MODE HAS 15 BODY PARTS, WITH MORE MOVEMENT AND A CRISPER FEEL.

**R6**  **R15**

Clothing ⌄    Body ⌄    Animations ⌄    Outfits ⌄

Body > Parts > Face

Body > Parts > Right arm

Body > Parts > Right leg

Clothing > Accessories > Hair

Clothing > Clothes > Shirts

Clothing > Clothes > Trousers

If you create a sick appearance that you love, save it in the **Outfits** tab. Then you can instantly select it again in the future.

Click or tap on your main avatar image, then move or drag it around to take a look at yourself from any camera angle!

Go to **Catalog** and select **Clothing**. This has a list of things like shirts and pants that can be altered to give your avatar a fresh look!

Remember you can pay with ROBUX to change your clothes, but the best (and free!) way to do this is to sort items in the **Relevance** tab from low to high price. You can now see all the free pants, shirts and other clothes.

Don't forget to play around with things like **Gear** and **Accessories**. These give you cool hairstyles, hats and extra items to wear or have in ROBLOX.

If you like something and it's free, or if you have enough Robux, click **Get** and then **Edit Avatar** to select it from your inventory.

# A WORLD OF CHOICE

With your player ready, take a look at the types of games and worlds to join!

## ROLE PLAY

One of the biggest types of game is role playing (RPG). Your avatar can join adventurous worlds and explore massive environments. You may have to complete missions, find and collect items, or escape capture. RPGs can be like real life too, and be set around working, eating and sleeping. Sound boring? Nothing is boring in ROBLOX!

👍 **PLAY IF YOU...** want endless adventure and to explore at your own pace.

⭐ **GAMES TO TRY...** Jailbreak, Work at a Pizza Place, ROBLOX High School, Welcome to Bloxburg

## TOWN AND CITY

THE PLAZA BETA

Some games cross over categories. For example, Jailbreak and Work at a Pizza Place can be classed as town and city and also role play. In town and city you'll find your way through built-up environments, tackle quests and interact with lots of other people.

👍 **PLAY IF YOU...** want a fun mix of RPG, exploring and adventure.

⭐ **GAMES TO TRY...** Meep City, The Plaza Beta, Pacifico

# BUILDING

# PLAYER POWER

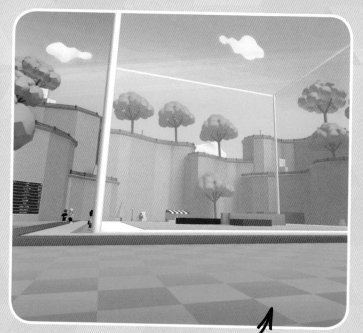

**BUILD BATTLE V2**

👍 **PLAY IF YOU...** really like building and want to become a pro!

⭐ **GAMES TO TRY...** Sandbox 1, Build Battle V2, Welcome to Bloxburg

Building is a gigantic part of ROBLOX so there are stacks of construction-based games! Once you've had a go in the ROBLOX Studio area, search for a game that lets you build cool structures, be inventive and push your imagination.

## ROBLOX FACT!

You can't search for a specific genre or type of game, so you may need to spend time clicking on games and reading the descriptions.

# TYCOON

A type of game where players can build and run a business using money-making skills to earn rewards and upgrades. The range of businesses is enormous, from theme parks to restaurants and wood chopping sites to superhero profit-making games!

**LUMBER TYCOON 2**

👍 **PLAY IF YOU...** think you can earn lots of cash and cool stuff!

⭐ **GAMES TO TRY...** Restaurant Tycoon, Super Hero Tycoon, Lumber Tycoon 2

# SURVIVAL

Survival games are a mix of action, role play, building, and shooting games. The ultimate aim is to protect your character, complete missions, or reach a certain location. You'll need to be super resourceful and have a sharp brain to stay alive!

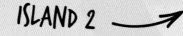 ISLAND 2

👍 **PLAY IF YOU...** like a challenge and taking on new environments and enemies.

- - - - - - - - - - - - - - - - - - - - - - - -

⭐ **GAMES TO TRY...** Natural Disaster Survival, Island 2, Booga Booga

# OBSTACLE

👍 **PLAY IF YOU...** fancy a bit of arcade style action!

- - - - - - - - - - - - - - - - - - - - - - - -

⭐ **GAMES TO TRY...** MEGA Challenge, Super Fun Easy Obstacle Course

Known as 'obby' games, these can either be speedy and complex, or a bit slow and silly. Your avatar may have to run, jump, dodge and duck to survive challenges and complete levels. It's awesome fun!

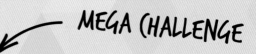 MEGA CHALLENGE

# FIRST PERSON SHOOTER

ROBLOX first person shooter (FPS) games are ultra popular! Phantom Forces rules this game genre and it lets players sneak around maps and take down enemies. Draw your weapon, lock the targets and start bossing locations!

## NERF FP2

👍 **PLAY IF YOU...** want fast-moving action and enjoy games like Fortnite!

⭐ **GAMES TO TRY...** Phantom Forces, Nerf FPS, Zombie Attack

# SIMULATOR

From driving, mining or robots to shopping or rocket launching – there's a simulator game to suit every gamer out there! Put your avatar in real-life or ridiculous situations and quickly master the powers you need to survive, progress and earn rewards!

# ADVENTURE

## HEROES OF ROBLOXIA

If you fancy a quick ten-minute blast or a longer quest-based mission, just search for an epic adventure title and you'll get a big boost of gaming adrenaline! From thrilling solo games to top team-based action, the adventure can take you anywhere.

## SPEED SIMULATOR

👍 **PLAY IF YOU...** want to be a hero and complete tricky tasks.

⭐ **GAMES TO TRY...** Heroes of Robloxia, Apocalypse Rising

👍 **PLAY IF YOU...** want to take control and gain some unusual user experience!

⭐ **GAMES TO TRY...** Mining Simulator, Vehicle Simulator, Speed Simulator

# STAY IN CONTROL

On Xbox, PC, Mac, tablet or phone, you'll need to master the main ROBLOX controls and functions.

## ON THE MENU

If you're an Xbox gamer and forget what the controls are during a game, just press the menu button on your controller. Then go to **settings** and the **help** tab to remind yourself of what the main move, toggle and tool buttons are.

## CONSOLE CHAT

On the Xbox version there is a voice chat system which lets players talk with their friends using a microphone headset. You can also hook up to the Xbox Live Party Chat and speak with your mates!

## LAPTOP LOOK

For PC and Mac gamers, go to the menu button and hit **Help**. This will display your character movement buttons, tool functions, and how to call up the main screens and other cool stuff.

## EPIC EMOTES

The animation system in ROBLOX lets your avatar pull out some flashy dances and basic emotes. In the in-game chat, type **/e dance2** or **/e dance3** to see an example of two rockin' routines!

## 'I' KNOW HOW TO MOVE!

On an iPad or iPhone there are two main buttons that control your avatar. Move the joystick in the bottom left corner of the screen to move your player. Tap the player icon on the other side and your character will jump. To attack an enemy just tap the screen in the location you want to go or cause damage!

## LIGHTS, CAMERA, ACTION!

ROBLOX has two main camera settings, called **Classic** and **Follow**. You can switch between the two in-game, and set it to the view you like best. **Classic** fixes the camera in one position and **Follow** rotates around your avatar.

## PACK YOUR BACKPACK

Access your **gear**, which are ROBLOX items to use in games, by clicking the backpack icon in the top left of the screen. When the backpack appears, you can access your inventory through a range of quick **'hotkeys'**.

# ROBUX AND BADGES

**1** This icon at the top of your main screen shows you how much Robux you have and the button that takes you to the **Buy Robux** area.

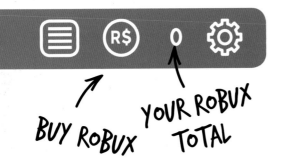

*BUY ROBUX*

*YOUR ROBUX TOTAL*

**2** If you're a member of the paid-for Builders Club scheme, you'll get 15 Robux given to you every day. Ker-ching!

**3** Badges show things that you've accomplished in ROBLOX. They can be won in-game for completing tasks or levels, or by connecting with the awesome ROBLOX world!

**4** To see the badges you have, go to your inventory and click on the badges tab. Click on each badge to remind you how you picked up the award.

**5** Builders Club members can create and upload their own special badges into games they create.

*BUILDERS CLUB BADGE*

### ROBLOX FACT!
Join the Turbo Builders Club to get 35 Robux each day, or the Outrageous Builders Club for 60 Robux!

*OUTRAGEOUS BUILDERS CLUB BADGE*

**6** The affiliate program is a smart way to earn extra Robux. If you share a link to something you like and a new user joins Robux from your link, you'll earn 5% of any Robux that person buys. Clever!

**7** ROBLOX developers can create game passes and sell them for Robux. If you're not a Builders Club member you'll get 10% of the Robux price of the pass. Game passes can unleash a special power or sick skills!

**8** It costs 100 Robux to create a badge, so make sure you design something you like and don't waste your cash!

**9** To see badges on offer in a game, click on the game and view badges in the **about** section. You'll see all the info you need, including any rare MVP awards.

**10** Never click on a link or visit a website that says it will give you free Robux or upgrades. Never enter your ROBLOX password other than on the official ROBLOX login page.

## MORE BADGES TO LOOK OUT FOR!

### FRIENDSHIP BADGE

Make 20 or more friends to pocket this award.

### HOMESTEAD BADGE

Earned when your personal place has clocked over 100 visits.

### ADMINISTRATOR BADGE

Shows an account is from an official ROBLOX admin person.

### VETERAN BADGE

For being a ROBLOX member for over a year.

# SHARING, SOCIAL AND SAFETY

Being social and sharing experiences in ROBLOX is great fun, but staying safe online is the most important thing.

ALL YOUR SETTINGS ARE HERE!

## USERNAME

Never use a player's **first name and surname** together when creating a Roblox username. Personal details, including address, email, phone number and school name, should never be shared on social media or revealed in text or voice chat.

NEVER SHARE YOUR PERSONAL DETAILS ONLINE!

## ROBLOX FACT!

Parents can set a four-digit PIN to keep privacy (chat and message) settings locked.

## ACCURATE INFO

Be sure to enter the player's true date of birth. This determines if they are placed in the under or over 13 years old category. A player's age is shown on the home page, next to their avatar name. 13+ means they are 13 or older and <13 shows they are 12 or younger.

## LANGUAGE FILTER

ROBLOX uses a very responsible and sophisticated filter system to restrict bad language and personal data being shared. Players under 12 are automatically registered to an even stronger filtering programme.

## REPORT IT

The game encourages users to report any poor or inappropriate behavior. This can be done by contacting **safety@roblox.com** or by clicking the various report buttons that appear around the homepage or during a game. Clicking on the flag next to a player's name is an easy way to report them to ROBLOX.

## SOCIAL NETWORKS

Social media sharing links, including YouTube, Twitter and Facebook, can also be restricted or controlled through the social networks area of the settings tab.

## CHAT SETTINGS

Go to the account settings page to check the status of people who can chat with you. Players 12 or younger can only communicate with other gamers they have accepted as friends. Parents who set up their child's account can also set it so that the player can accept no friend requests.

## BLOCKING

ROBLOX allows users to block others from chatting to you, including blocking someone while a game is being played. This is done by either going to that user's profile page or by selecting them on the in-game leaderboard.

# ROCKIN' ROBLOX GAMES!

The most epic thing about ROBLOX is the gazillions of games to choose from. The following 26 pages reveal the most amazing and wacky games to try out. From prisons to pizzas, meeps to mining and scuba diving to sandstorms, your gaming brains will be overloaded!

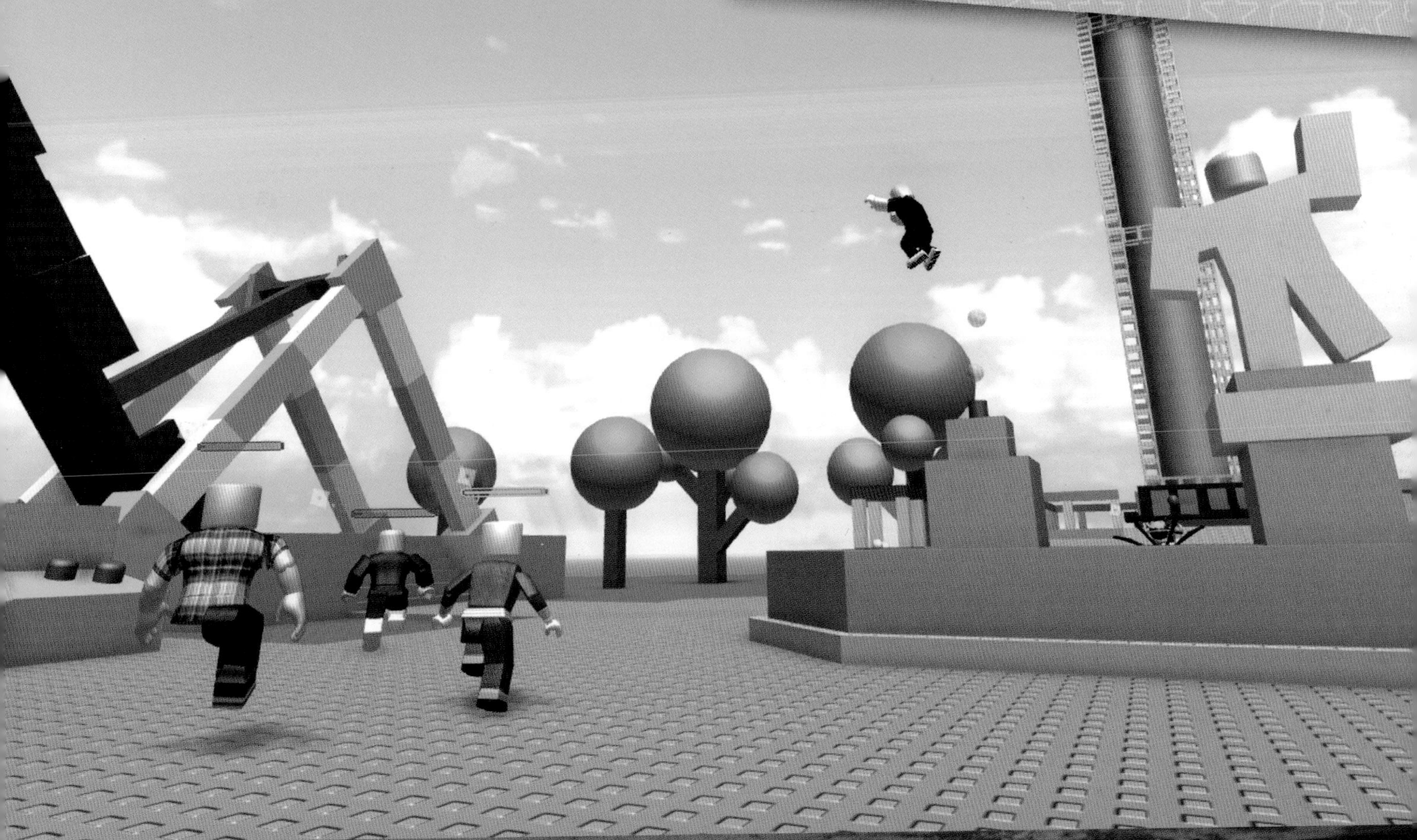

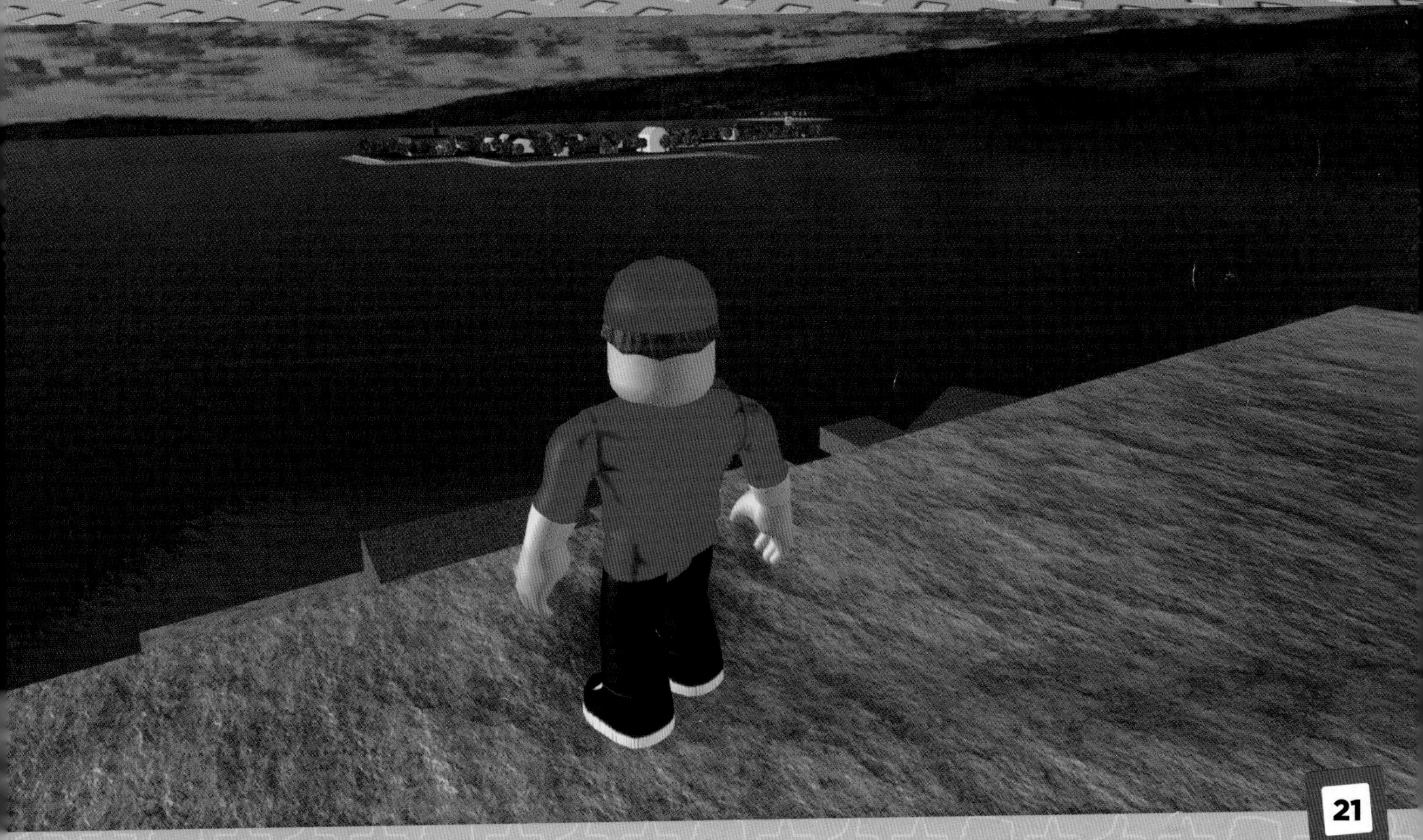

# JAILBREAK

Get inside the biggest ROBLOX game of all time. It's an action-packed cops-and-robbers fest!

Jailbreak has a gigantic ROBLOX following and over 100,000 users can play at once. It's a simple and fun game and can be played at a frantic or medium pace, depending on what you fancy! You can either team up with friends or go solo, and you get the choice of being a prisoner or a police officer.

BE A PRISONER...

...OR A POLICE OFFICER

Being a prisoner is way more exciting! You'll need to bust out of jail, which can be done by pickpocketing a key card from a cop, punching a fuse box to open the gate or even hijacking the prison helicopter! Once you're outside you'll be a crim on the run and the police will be hunting you!

Outside of the prison, criminals can cause carnage in the city! The bank and jewelry store have lots of loot to scoop, and the gas station and donut shop can be robbed, too. If you can land on top of the train, get into the red carriage and try to steal the cash inside!

The more bad stuff the criminals do, the higher their bounty level rises. The 'most wanted' board is displayed in the prison and police station, and officers who arrest the biggest bad guys collect that bounty. Slapping the handcuffs on is a cop's top aim!

LET'S GET THEM!

**Most Wanted**

| | | | |
|---|---|---|---|
| kylejc259 $1,800 Bounty | | ZorvPvP $1,600 Bounty | |
| eneskoydu $1,050 Bounty | | killmonger888 $200 Bounty | |

Arrest these criminals & earn their bounties!

👍 **VISITS:** 1 billion+ (as of June 2018)

🔧 **CREATED:** September 2017

👤 **CREATED BY:** Badimo

⭐ **GENRE:** Town and City/RPG

**MAXIMUM PLAYERS:** 26

# JAILBREAK

This adventurous RPG game is really easy to get to grips with. Escaping the prison is just the start – beyond that fence there's a city full of things to rob! Firstly, head to the city criminal base or the secret mountain base. There you can uncover weapons, pick up a cool car and change from your prison jumpsuit.

## UNDERGROUND INFO

The crazy sewer escape update was released in 2018, with escape ladders from the stinky sewers in the prison. Watch out though, because not all of them will get you outside the perimeter!

## ZOOM IN

Climb the radio tower in the city to find the secret binoculars. You'll then have a close-up view of the whole city!

### BE CAREFUL

Punching stuff, exploding walls and climbing towers will attract the guards' attention! If you play as a police officer, you're tasked with keeping crims inside the prison, making arrests and stopping jailbreakers from rampaging the city.

# BLINGIN' BUGATTI

The Bugatti Veyron is the fastest car in Jailbreak. It costs a mega $500,000 and has an unlimited top speed. Police cars are slightly quicker than crim cars, but they won't catch a Bugatti!

## OUT OF THIS WORLD

In the meteor by the $1M Dealership, you can find the cool alien UFO. It's small and speedy and if you get inside this futuristic machine you'll be flying through tiny gaps and away from the law!

## MEGA MONEY

Play Jailbreak as a police officer and you'll get a $500 paycheck every morning and $200 for arresting prisoners and crims. That's why the cops are quick to catch offenders!

Robbing the jewellery store is a smart move, but don't forget there are two giant moneybags on the top level of the store. So dodge the lasers and pick up that cash!

Buying the bigger duffel bag means that crims can cram up to three times more stolen stuff inside it when robbing the bank. Splashing cash on the new bag could be worth it in the long run!

# WORK AT A PIZZA PLACE

Pepperoni or cheese and tomato fans need to get a slice of this mega popular game! Take a look at what this fun place is all about.

**WHAT JOB WILL YOU TAKE?**

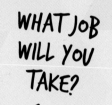

Jump into the world of pizzas and straight away you must pick a job. These are cashier, cook, pizza-boxer, delivery and supplier. Or you could start by creating and furnishing your house, which will be located close to the pizza place. Players earn 'moneyz' and paychecks from doing their work to buy stuff and upgrade their homes.

You also have the chance to be the pizza place manager, which is pretty cool! Just go and sit in the manager's office chair while the job is vacant. But be a good boss and treat your workers fairly, or they could vote you out!

## ROBLOX FACT!

Players are 'on break' if they enter a house or do nothing while working. Taking a break means no paycheck!

## CASHIER

New players often like to work as the cashier. This job means you're the first person to greet non-playable customers (NPCs) and you need to take orders by asking questions and entering info on the keypad. Mess this job up and the cook, boxer, and delivery worker are affected too!

## WORKING IN THE KITCHEN

Pay attention if you're the cook because there is a lot to do. First check what the orders are on the board and make the right flavour pizza to cook in the oven – it will ping to let you know it's ready. Take out the pizza before it burns or you'll need the fire extinguisher! And if you leave a dropped pizza on the floor, bugs might crawl over it.

## CAR PARK

Take the pizza delivery or supplier job if you like driving. Cars can spawn around the pizza parlor car park, so take a quick drive around the town to check out where the main locations are. Delivering is easy because a yellow arrow leads you to the customer's house.

👍 **VISITS:** 786 million

🔧 **CREATED:** March 2008

👤 **CREATED BY:** Dued1

⭐ **GENRE:** Town and City

**MAXIMUM PLAYERS:** 12

Art by XtreamHunter76

ROBLOX WORK AT A PIZZA PLACE

# WORK AT A PIZZA PLACE

These helpful hints will get you bossing this game! Work at a Pizza Place is all about teamwork. If you don't work, or if you behave poorly towards the others in your server, the manager and staff can take action against you. So take a job quickly and get to business!

## PIZZA BASE

Join Work at a Pizza Place and you're given your own house in a random location on the island. It's small and basic to start with, but use your earned Moneyz to search the catalogue and add cool upgrades like furniture, paintings and a backyard. There's even a glamorous Mansion to buy for a huge 3,000 Robux!

## MONEY MAKING

Being a cashier can be a low paid job. Cooking the pizzas brings in more cash, but it may be busy in the kitchen if other gamers make that choice too!

IN THE MANAGER'S OFFICE YOU CAN OPEN THE BLINDS BY CLICKING ON THEM – GOOD FOR SPYING ON YOUR STAFF!

## MANAGER MAYHEM

Keep an eye on the player menu on the right of the screen. It shows what jobs people have – if there's no manager listed and you want the role, rush to the manager's office!

**SECRET ROOM THIS WAY...**

## JUMP THRU

Don't miss the secret room, which has an entrance near the drive thru. Jump through the darker brick pattern and you can spy on lots of your co-workers!

## ALL SMILES

Click on the smiley face button and your avatar can dance, move, laugh, cry, speak and do a whole bunch of cool things!

## BARGAIN BUYS

When it's open, the dump building that's close to the pizza shop is an awesome place to pick up cheap items for your house. It's one of the best ways to upgrade your home and then attract visitors.

## SWIM FOR CASH

Swim out to the small island and you'll easily find a hidden treasure chest with 1,500 moneyz! To swim, make sure **detailed water** is switched on in your settings, otherwise you'll sink and it'll be game over!

## ISLAND ITEMS

Swim or glide out to the other distant island and you'll meet a man outside a small hut. You can sell furniture items to him and raise some much-needed moneyz!

## ROBLOX FACT!

Buy the glider in-game through the shopping cart button and you'll reach the island much quicker.

# MINING SIMULATOR

It's time to go underground and understand all the block, ore and mining abilities in this special simulator game!

**COLLECT SOME COINS**

Mining Simulator blasted into (and underneath!) the ROBLOX world in 2018. The aim is to mine below ground for blocks of different materials, called ores, and collect coins to upgrade your character with new tools and backpacks. You start with a basic pickaxe and a small backpack. Get bashing blocks quickly in the Mine area to gather coins and buy more helpful items!

**The Mine**

**START DIGGING**

Mining grass or dirt has a coin value of 1, but clay, stone, copper and obsidian have much higher values. Mine the precious ores to make serious cash! Once your backpack is full, return to the surface to sell your mined materials and buy stuff. Spend wisely and you'll soon see your blocks and coin stash rocket!

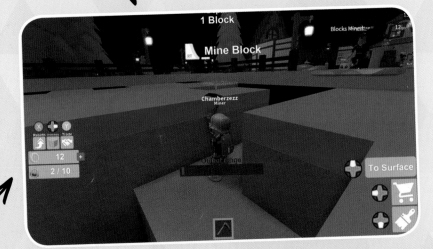

**LET'S BUY STUFF!**

Click on the codes button for a clever way to instantly get more coins! Codes can be found by searching online, and other gamers often share the most valuable ones. They can expire so you have to keep looking for working codes and you can only use them once.

TIME TO START SELLING

Pets and hats are two upgrades that are very helpful in Mining Simulator. Pets follow behind you and have the ability to increase your mining speed, power and ore value. Get a hat from a hat crate or by trading with another player to boost your mining skills. A mythical hat, like storm dominus, will increase power by 750!

## ROBLOX FACT!

Some hats also increase jump power.

Collecting 10 million coins sounds like a big task, but once you've done it you can 'rebirth' and push up your ore value by x2 each time. It's an epic way to level up your materials each time you rebirth. But you do lose the tools, backpacks and coins you've earned. Pets, hats, eggs, crates and skins will remain in your inventory after each rebirth.

YOU KEEP YOUR PETS AFTER REBIRTH!

👍 **VISITS:** 161 million

🔧 **CREATED:** September 2017

👤 **CREATED BY:** Runway Rumble

⭐ **GENRE:** Mining / all genres

**MAXIMUM PLAYERS:** 10

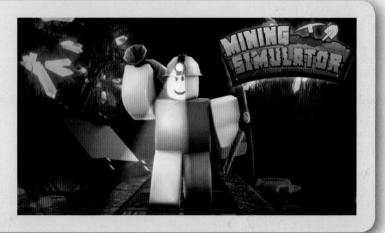

# MINING SIMULATOR

Finding a code to collect your first hat and pet is a smart way to start using these game-boosting items. It could take an hour or two of constant mining and selling to collect enough coins to make an impact in this simulator. Keep an eye on the player table at the top of the screen to see how your numbers compare to the others in your server.

## REBIRTH REWARDS

Rebirth tokens are awarded after a rebirth. Go to the rebirth shop and pick up eggs (which spawn pets), crates and previously locked backpacks and tools. Tokens can also be bought with Robux.

POP TO THE REBIRTH SHOP!

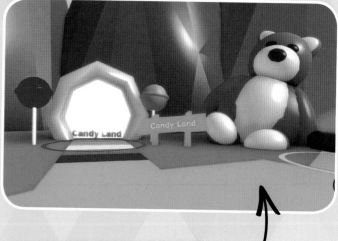

## SWEET SUCCESS

After your first rebirth, make sure you enter the candy land mine. The regular stone here is replaced with sugar stone, which has a better coin value. Say hi to the gingerbread NPCs, too!

## QUEST CATCH-UP

In the main gaming area, keep checking in with Quinn to see how far through each quest you are. Crates and eggs are often awarded for finishing your latest random quest.

# BOSS BACKPACK

Think about upgrading to the cylinder backpack once you've collected 200,000 coins. Its 8,500 storage will keep you underground for a long time with no need for constant surface hopping!

*BOSSING IT!*

# JUMP IN

Making your own mines will teach you the game basics, but jumping into another player's mine could get you deeper much quicker! Watch out though as specialist tools will be needed to get through tougher materials in lower levels.

## TOP TRADING

Get to know the trade tool. You can select which other player to trade with, and try to tempt them to give up something mega from their inventory in return for an object from yours.

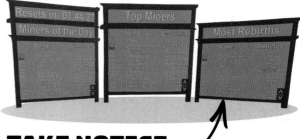

## TAKE NOTICE

Take a look at these notice boards in Mining Simulator. Aim to become the best miner of the day and always check your rank – insane miner or higher is incredible!

## ROBLOX FACT!

The mine will collapse and fall in when the area's been dug up. You'll have to wait for it to re-spawn.

*SPACE ADVENTURE LAND*

*FOOD LAND!*

## BEST CHESTS

Be alert and spot treasure chests underground! Wood and silver are very common, but keep mining and you could locate something rare like a shadow chest – it has a base value of 60,000 coins!

# SCUBA DIVING AT QUILL LAKE

Get your diving gear on and splash around in this special scuba ROBLOX adventure!

Dive for coins, artifacts and treasures so that you can earn cash to upgrade your diving gear. Suits, boats, air tanks, jackets, weights and training are all on offer if you have the money!

## ROBLOX FACT!

Got 400 Robux to spare? Buy the aquabreather and you'll never run out of air.

The flashlight's a must-buy item early on in Scuba Diving at Quill Lake. It's helpful underwater and in the dark and dangerous Union Railworld camp tunnels.

At the start of a game, pick up the power suit schematics from the top of the tower that's close to the two mountainside tunnels. You'll also need power suit scrap, a cell from a sunken ship and lava reactor to put the suit together.

DISCOVER TREASURE!

## VISIT STEVE'S CRAB SHACK

👍 **VISITS:** 26 million

🔧 **CREATED:** September 2010

👤 **CREATED BY:** ColonelGraff

⭐ **GENRE:** Adventure

🧍 **MAXIMUM PLAYERS:** 10

The geolocator in Steve's Scuba Shop will show your coordinates. That's mega helpful when you're diving to track down items like the dragonbone crown and blue jade necklace at the bottom of the water.

## SNEAK ON TO A BOAT

If you're trying to get back to shore and don't have a dinghy boat, you may be able to hop on a boat that's not moving and get yourself a cheeky free ride!

Sometimes coins can be found high up on the rocks around Quill Lake. Master the art of climbing and jumping, then keep your eyes peeled for sparkling money!

# HIDE AND SEEK EXTREME

It's so simple, but so much fun! Hide from the 'IT' character in this speedy and exciting game!

When a random map is chosen, such as the kitchen, attic, store or cupboard, the game selects who will be the 'IT' character and challenged with finding the other 12 hiders.

ROOM SELECTION

SEEKER FROZEN WHILE COUNTING!

After spawning, the hiders have one minute to run and find a place to disguise themselves. The chase then begins when the seeker is unfrozen and starts exploring the location!

YOU'RE 'IT'!

**HIDING PLACE**

Click the **Spectate IT** button to see what IT is up to and whether they are heading your way. Spin the camera around to get a better view. The 'studs away' counter displays the distance between IT and you.

**SPECTATE IT BUTTON**

## ROBLOX FACT!

IT must touch you to put you out of the game. If you're hiding in a high place and IT closes in, try jumping down to escape from them.

**STUDS AWAY COUNTER**

Watch out, because IT can use abilities like glue, sprint and special cameras to track down hiders! The glue can only be used when IT is close to you, but it'll slow you down.

At the beginning of the game, try to collect coins which will be randomly placed around the location. Coins can be used to upgrade your character. You will also get credits if you survive the game without being caught.

Listen out for nearby footsteps when you're hiding. This could mean that the seeker's right on your tail!

**VISITS:** 309 million

**CREATED:** January 2015

**CREATED BY:** Tim7775

**GENRE:** Adventure

**MAXIMUM PLAYERS:** 14

# VEHICLE SIMULATOR

Race, cruise, customize or collect – Vehicle Simulator is one of the top motoring games on ROBLOX!

Newcomers to this action-packed driving sim should play as a citizen. This will help you get to grips with the game and basic controls. Most importantly, you should know how to scroll around your cellphone and its main functions.

There are four types of vehicles to choose from; cars, boats, planes and utility. Enter a dealership to see what your cash will let you buy.

## FIND A DEALERSHIP

## CHECK OUT YOUR CELLPHONE

16:12

Money is earned by driving through the city, racing and completing quests and task. As well as upgrading and customizing your motor, players can buy a house, too.

Police, SWAT and Tow Trucker jobs will give you missions to master, and the chance to rack up cash. Being a cop isn't easy – the NPC crims are always up to no good and ready to speed away before you can arrest them!

In the dealership you can take super cars, like a Ferrari and Lamborghini, on short test drives for free. While driving at high speed you'll make more money. Simple!

## COOL STUNTS

## CUSTOMIZE YOUR CAR

**VISITS:** 194 million

**CREATED:** August 2014

**CREATED BY:** Simbuilder

**GENRE:** Town and City

**MAXIMUM PLAYERS:** 18

Performing stunts, winning drag races and doing track laps will earn you money. There are also badges to collect – pick up 50 race wins to become a track master!

# MEEPCITY

## ROBLOX FACT!
Hit the red home button to instantly teleport yourself to your estate.

**One of the biggest RPG/Town and City games in the history of ROBLOX, MeepCity is packed with fun and adventure!**

Hang out with friends, upgrade your house, go fishing, play mini games and become best buds with your own Meep pet. That's what MeepCity is all about! Jump into the main playground lobby and there are loads of game options, like entering the town, neighborhood or plaza.

## FISHING AT THE PIER

You can go fishing in lots of waterside spots. Stand on an empty pier, cast your rod and aim to hook up a fish. Different fish are worth different levels of coins. When your bucket is full, it can be sold at the fish shop for coins.

## VISIT THE STAR BALL

GAME
STAR BALL

The pet shop is also where you can adopt a Meep. These are cute, bouncy creatures that follow you around and can be customized, named and even given beds, houses and food bowls. Cuteness overload!

## ADOPT A MEEP!

Playing mini games is one of the coolest things in MeepCity. Star Ball is found in the town and is a skillful game where you role your Meep around different courses, racing to collect stars. Dash to the plaza for a game of MeepCity kart racing with friends!

## ROBLOX FACT!

Win a kart race and you'll collect a cool prize!

## KART RACING AT AT THE PLAZA

Don't forget to join a party inside your friends' houses! Here you'll get food, music and the chance to hang out with cool people. Make your own house stand out by planting pretty flowers outside. Don't forget to water them! Flowers can also be sold to raise cash.

👍 **VISITS:** 1 billion+

🔧 **CREATED:** February 2016

👤 **CREATED BY:** alex newtron

⭐ **GENRE:** Town and City

🤖 **MAXIMUM PLAYERS:** 100

# ZOMBIE ATTACK

**Just like the name says, this game is all about attacking zombies and defeating gross enemies with weapons!**

Working as a team, your job is to battle zombies that come at you in frenzied waves! Use your weapon to blast 'em and collect cash for each kill. Stay on the move and keep taking down the enemy so you can upgrade your basic pistol to something powerful, like an uzi or shotgun!

BOSS ZOMBIE

## ROBLOX FACT!

There are at least 12 maps in Zombie Attack, ranging from the prison to farm, factory and pyramid.

Every ten zombie waves you'll see one super zombie, called a boss. These creatures have immense power and get tougher with each level. Mega Tank bosses throw rocks, the Dark Ghost has red orbs and the mighty Dragon Beast has lasers and dragon breath!

You can level up during games by collecting epic items. Super speed will help you outrun the zombies, invincibility is the ultimate lifeline and exploding grenades can wipe out the monsters in one mega move.

Players complete missions to progress through levels and waves to get cash. Missions are based on your kill stats and for crushing different zombie types, such as sand, slime, lava and crystal.

**VISITS:** 176 million

**CREATED:** December 2017

**CREATED BY:** wenlocktoad vs indra

**GENRE:** All genres

**MAXIMUM PLAYERS:** 8

Top tips for staying out of zombie danger are jumping to high spots, shooting from a distance, using boxes to shield you, and keeping moving. Oh, and remember that zombies attack from any ground direction!

## ROBLOX FACT!

If you get defeated, you can have some fun and actually play as a zombie for the rest of that wave!

SAND ZOMBIE

VOID SLIME

LAVA ZOMBIE

# NATURAL DISASTER SURVIVAL

Storms, floods, fires and earthquakes could be heading your way in this all-action survival adventure!

## ROBLOX FACT!

Survive a power 7 multi-disaster to pick up the rarest badge in the game.

**Disaster Warning:**
Volcanic Eruption! Get away from the volcano

## GET AWAY FROM THE VOLCANO!

In each round of Natural Disaster Survival, a random map is chosen and players teleport to that location. After about 20 seconds a disaster warning will appear and you must decide what action to take to stay in the game! Yikes.

The types of disasters that can strike include acid rain, volcanic eruption, sandstorm, tornado, tsunami and meteor shower. The disaster warning is your early alert system, but look up to the skies and you could see clues to the start of thundery weather or a sand blast!

**Disaster Warning:**
Tornado! Stay clear of its path

## WATCH THE ACTION FROM THE TOWER

Need a lift?

Pick up a green balloon of your own!

Click Now!

Just 80 R$

As you wait in the lobby before each game, or while you respawn after being wiped out, head to the top of the tower. Here you can pick up a green balloon. This will help you rise quickly and descend safely. Only problem is that it costs Robux!

## THE WEATHER MACHINE

You can also use Robux to crank up the weather machine in the tower. This means you'll face multiple disasters at the same time and means your survival skills will be tested to the max!

## HEALTH BAR

Health

Health

Health

Keep an eye on your health bar at the top of the screen. You'll begin in the green, but will start to tip into red and your time in the game can quickly disappear!

👍 **VISITS:** 561 million

🔧 **CREATED:** March 2008

👤 **CREATED BY:** Stickmasterluke

⭐ **GENRE:** All genres

**MAXIMUM PLAYERS:** 30

# BEST OF THE REST!

## 2 PLAYER SUPERHERO TYCOON

Do battle with a friend and boss enemy teams and take control of your tycoon.

Attack other tycoon bases using weapons. Special items like the grapple hook help you zoom into action.

Watch out for superhero updates – The Incredibles made an appearance in 2018!

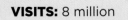 **VISITS:** 8 million

**CREATED:** June 2018

**GENRE:** All genres

## EPIC MINIGAMES

Choose from over 70 new, exciting quick-fire games. Users need to collect wins to level up.

Games will be based on player skill, slick moves, strategy... and even luck! They could be playing solo or in teams.

Earn coins for cooler gear, pets and items. In-game codes will boost you, too.

**VISITS:** 338 million

**CREATED:** July 2015

**GENRE:** All genres

## BOOGA BOOGA

Gamers must be sharp in the mind and strong in the arm – Booga Booga is a fierce island tribal survival quest!

Tribe chiefs need to build super-strong forts to keep rampaging intruders at bay.

Armor and weapons (ranged and melee) must all be upgraded and equipped to conquer enemies.

👍 **VISITS:** 140 million

🔧 **CREATED:** December 2017

⭐ **GENRE:** All genres

## PHANTOM FORCES

Deploy to the battlefield and hunt down enemies with your squad as the phantom and ghost teams go head to head!

Customize your weapon with skins, increase its power, damage and accuracy and keep track of weapon kill counts.

Destroy the most enemy numbers in each 15 minute shootout.

👍 **VISITS:** 443 million

🔧 **CREATED:** September 2015

⭐ **GENRE:** First Person Shooter

# 8 EPIC REASONS TO BEGIN BUILDING!

**1**
By using the **ROBLOX Studio** function you can pretty much build any 3D game experience you can imagine! Recreate a popular game or come up with a unique new idea. The options, location and missions are all up to you...

**2**
Join the paid-for ROBLOX Builders Club (BC) and get between 15 to 60 Robux awarded every day! BC also lets you sell and trade items and join and create ROBLOX discussion groups.

**3**
Building your own ROBLOX games and worlds is heaps of fun! If you love playing ROBLOX, you could enjoy creating just as much.

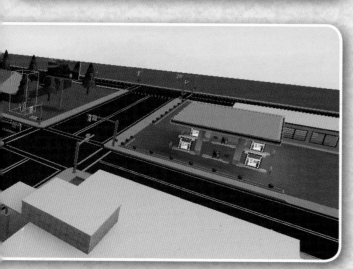

**4** Building and using **ROBLOX Studio** teaches you about computer functions, programs, and scripting. You'll upgrade your computer-savvy brain and develop your IT skills!

**5** You can create cool vehicles as well as buildings and natural features like lakes and hills with the **terrains** function.

**6** To learn the basics of creating, you can recreate real-life buildings that you know, like your own house or school!

**7** Your character will be the very first to test and explore your new game before you make a game public. Invite friends to have a go, too!

**8** Create special **game passes** for your new world which will give players cool abilities or powers! BC members get more Robux rewards for each pass sold.

# GET TO KNOW
# ROBLOX STUDIO

**This is your window to the building world, with all the tabs and functions you need to get creating!**

Take time to fully explore the **ROBLOX Studio start page.** It will have tabs such as file, home and model across the top, plus project, explorer and properties panels which are usually in columns on each side of the start page.

The three templates tabs are very helpful for studio newcomers. There are empty baseplate and flat terrain templates, themed pre-built games and gameplay templates with custom features built-in.

CLICK HERE!

HAVE A BROWSE!

All Templates    Theme    Gameplay

| Baseplate | Flat Terrain | Village | Castle | Suburban | Racing |

| Pirate Island | Western | City | Obby | Starting Place | |

| Infinite Runner | Capture The Flag | Team/FFA Arena | Combat | Volcanic Island | |

## ROBLOX FACT!
If something in toolbox has a little orange shield, it means it's a very good item to pick.

TOOLBOX ITEMS

INTERFACE

PLAY BUTTON

EXPLORER BOX

The tutorials panel, which often displays on the bottom left of your screen, is super useful to learn simple instructions around building a game and has items like trees, doors, cars and rivers.

The **select**, **move**, **scale** and **rotate** buttons are great for positioning and building parts and simple to use. Practise using them on random objects you've put on your template.

With lots of pre-made stuff to choose from, the **toolbox** is a must for both beginners and pros, too! It saves you having to create complicated items, and at the click of a button, your world can have things like roads, schools, houses, machines, a city... even zombies! Use the scroll down menu to search categories or type a specific item you're after.

## ROBLOX FACT!

Studio operates on PC and Mac computers, but any PC or Mac-created game can be played across smartphones, tablets and consoles.

Click the **test button** and your character will appear in the world you've created. It's the best way to experience what the gameplay is like.

**Explorer** is a big box that looks a bit complicated at first! Here it shows you where all of your project files are. Click on something and more details will appear in **properties** underneath it. As you build, practise using these two boxes. To start with you can make a simple baseplate bigger by increasing its size.

# GAME ON!

**It's your turn to start creating games, beginning with a simple obstacle course.**

If you've played the obby in gameplay templates you'll know the basic things needed for an obstacle course are jumping to levels and platforms and moving around. Open **workspace** in the **explorer** window, click on **baseplate** and then hit your delete button. This will create an empty world for you to make your first obby game!

You'll need to make a **spawn location** to mark your game's starting point – otherwise players will drop to their death! Open the **+** button beside workspace, then scroll down and click on **spawn location**. A tile with a black circle and sun-like rays will appear in your empty world.

FILE MENU

TAB BETWEEN HOME, MODEL, TEST AND VIEW WINDOWS

EXPLORER WINDOW

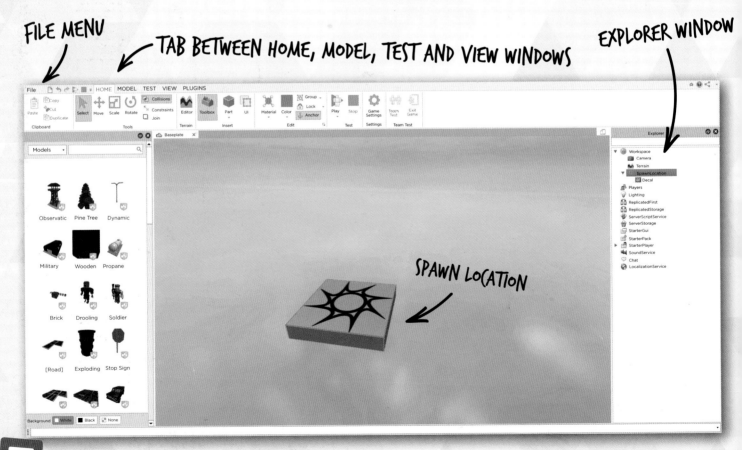

SPAWN LOCATION

In the **model** tab, click on **part** and then choose a block, sphere, wedge or cylinder to appear in your game. Control where and how big you want the part by using the **move** and **scale** tool.

You need to **anchor** blocks and parts to stop them falling. Make sure you're in the model tab, then highlight the part and click **anchor**, which is next to the surface option.

Also in the model tab is **collisions.** When this is on it'll be greyed out and means that parts won't be able to overlap each other.

Keep adding to your obstacle course with more blocks and parts. Make them different sizes and at different levels.

In the home tab, click on **play.** Here you can test your game to check it's working properly and that you can jump between the bricks.

## ROBLOX FACT!

Add effects like fire and smoke to your parts in the game by right clicking on a part in the explorer tab.

MOVE AND SCALE TOOLS

COLLISIONS BUTTON

PLAY BUTTON

PART TOOL

ANCHOR BUTTON

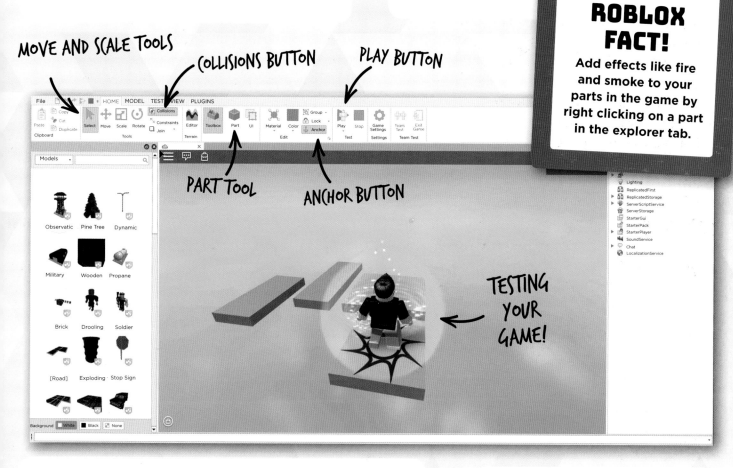

TESTING YOUR GAME!

It's good to add a **checkpoint** so that if a player falls off, they'll rejoin at that point and not at the start. In the model tab click **service,** then **teams** and **insert.** This brings up **teams** in the explorer panel, which you should right click, then select **insert object** and **team.** Name that object, then select a colour and place it on your map after selecting **spawn** at the top of your page.

You've now created your first simple game! Keep play testing it and make sure you regularly save and **publish to ROBLOX** to keep all of your edits.

# YOUR WORLD

**Take control and build the ultimate place to let your ROBLOX dreams come true!**

**BUILD A LANDSCAPE!**

Building and creating your first **ROBLOX world** is more complicated than an obby game, but you'll get the hang of it after a few hours in Studio. This time start with the **flat terrain** template.

The **terrain** editor tool in the home tab is a fantastic feature to quickly build a landscape. When you're inside this function, click **generate** and choose the biomes you want. Select things like mountains, hills and water, and then tap **generate** at the bottom to create your world!

**TERRAIN GENERATE BUTTON**

**TERRAIN EDITOR**

**TERRAIN GENERATOR SETTINGS**

Play around in terrain editor with the **add, subtract, paint** and **smooth** buttons. These will make your world even better and just as you imagined it would be!

## ROBLOX FACT!

Just like when you set up your obby game, remember to keep saving and publishing to ROBLOX.

Now try adding new terrain to a different template, like **village, castle** or **pirate island.** Use the **toolbox** to quickly add items and buildings to your environment.

In the **test** tab, select **play** to let your avatar experience what it's like to interact in your awesome world!

Use the **copy** and **paste** options, on the top left of your Studio start page, to speed up your building. This lets you create a street of repeat buildings, or the same vehicle throughout a town. You can always edit or scale pre-made buildings to make them look different!

*TEST TAB*

*PLAY BUTTON*

*COPY AND PASTE OPTIONS*

*TOOLBOX ITEMS*

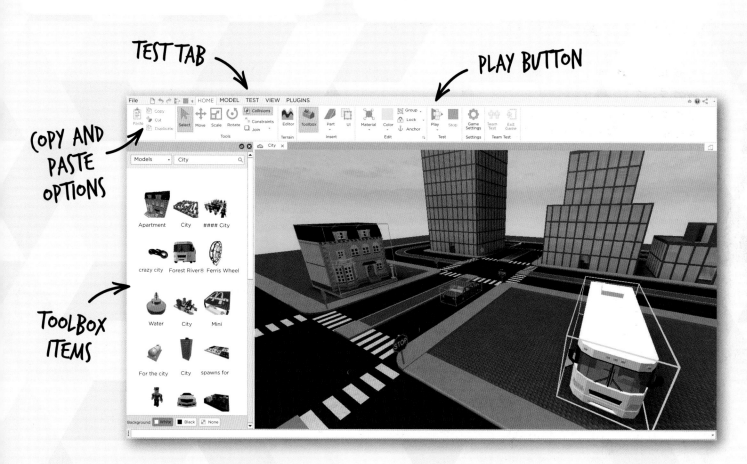

**Scripting** in ROBLOX is the commands given to blocks and parts which tell them to do certain things or act a certain way. Scripting allows NPCs to walk, other cars to drive, words to appear on screen, items to deal damage, and lots more!

Scripting requires a programming language called **Lua.** In the **view** tab, click **tutorials** and you'll find basic official ROBLOX scripting guides to teach you about inserting Lua script into your games and worlds.

# TIPS & TRICKS

Discover some epic ways to be a boss builder in ROBLOX!

 **1** Include your own 2D images in your builds, like on the side of walls or as posters. In **view** tab, click **game explorer** to open it. Then right click on **assets** to add an image from your computer.

 **3** Light up your game! Select cool lighting, such as sun rays and blur, from **effects** in the explorer's advanced objects setting.

 **2** Pressing your **control** keyboard button and **1, 2, 3** or **4**, toggles you between the **select, move, scale** and **rotate** tools quickly. **Control** and **D**, and **control** and **F**, are useful duplicate and camera control **hotkeys**.

**4** Practise with the **union, negate** and **separate** tools in the model tab to create structures that can merge or be pulled apart.

 **5** Keep players coming back to your game by updating it with new levels and features!

## ROBLOX FACT!

Use the My Decals dropdown list in toolbox to quickly find any images you've used.

**8** Adding a fun **text label** to parts is easy. Go to **insert object** in that part's explorer tab, then **surfaceGui** to insert a label.

**9** Create a **spinning brick** in an obstacle course! Anchor a brick, add a **motor** to it from the surface function in the model tab, then put an unanchored brick on top. Click run from the home tab and watch it spin!

**6** If you create a multiplayer game for lots of users, place different **spawn location** tiles. Then players will appear at different points in the game and not together in a bunch.

**7** In the view tab, the **context help** button could get you a quick on-line answer to a ROBLOX question you have.

# POPULAR POWER!

Now you can build games, worlds and places, you need to know how to make it stand out on ROBLOX.

## EPIC ICON

There are thousands of games on the ROBLOX site, but a sick game icon will help get you noticed. It needs to show exactly what your game is, plus look exciting and adventurous!

IT'S ALL ABOUT THE ICON!

[NEW!] EGG FARM
18,143 Playing

MeepCity
17,354 Playing

Bee Swarm Sim...
16,473 Playing

[PAINT] Adopt Me!
14,677 Playing

Phantom Forces
14,439 Playing

Welcome to Bloxburg
14,370 Playing

Royale High
9,156 Playing

Vechile Simulator
8,300 Playing

Work at a Pizza Place
6,870 Playing

Robloxian High...
6,325 Playing

Granny [FIX]
6,164 Playing

Murder Mystery 2
5,749 Playing

[Quests!] Build A B...
4,835 Playing

Super Hero Tycoon
4,326 Playing

Lumber Tycoon 2
4,317 Playing

[ ] HEAVY PISTOL!]
4,278 Playing

## ROBLOX FACT!

Icons also appear on your profile page and favourites lists, with a maximum dimension of 512x512 pixels.

58

## THUMBS UP

Game developers can use as many as five thumbnail images to promote their creations on the game page. These can be automatically generated, but your game will appeal more with custom thumbnails. Try to include a video, too!

[🎉HEAVY PISTOL!]
Island Royale - Beta
By **LordJurrd**

Play

⭐ 417K+  👍 124K+  16K+ 👎

## YOUTUBE RULES

Why not add your own YouTube video to the gallery? It'll show exactly what your game is about and attract ROBLOX fans to check it out. This will cost 500 Robux and can be a maximum of 30 seconds.

## PASS IT ON

Create top-class game passes for users to buy with Robux to keep them coming back to your game! Passes also need a good 150x150 pixels icon. See the robloxdev.com site for steps on how to make a game pass.

## SUPER SELL

The words you use to describe your game under the thumbnails is vital. It's your chance to make the game sound amazing! Give detail in the description, but use short and exciting sentences. Take time to get it just right!

## ROBLOX FACT!

Some more advanced developers can use Robux to pay for adverts that promote their games.

## SOCIAL SCENE

Telling others about your builds and games in ROBLOX forums will attract people to play it. Ask users for their thoughts and ideas for how your game could be made even better. If you make cool upgrades, share this on your ROBLOX social channels and tell your friends.

# ROBLOX BRAIN BUSTERS!

Think your head's overloaded with ROBLOX stats and info?
Take the test, then turn over to find out your score!

**1** Which of these are real ROBLOX games?

A. **Phantom Farce**

B. **Zombie Rush**

C. **Royale Mining High**

**2** How many hours did ROBLOX gamers play, in total, between 2008-2018?

A. **14 million**

B. **400 billion**

C. **14 billion**

**3** What's another name for a player's character in the game?

A. **Avatar**

B. **Aviator**

C. **Radiator**

**4** What do we call business-based games where players aim to earn money?

A. **Survival**

B. **Tycoon**

C. **Trading**

**5** Do you know what the term FPS stands for?

A **First person shooter**

B. **Firing person strategy**

C. **Fling poison strangely**

**6** What does this ROBLOX symbol represent?

A. **Friend requests**

B. **Game badge rarity**

C. **Robux**

**7** What was the first game to reach 1 billion visits?

A. **Meep City**

B. **ROBLOXian High School**

C. **Vehicle Simulator**

**8** Which of these is not a real Work at a Pizza Place job?

A. **Cook**

B. **Cleaner**

C. **Supplier**

**9** What's the part of ROBLOX.com where game building happens?

A. **Office**

B. **Shop**

C. **Studio**

**10** What was ROBLOX originally called?

A. **Robotblox**

B. **Dynablocks**

C. **Box of Blox**

**11** In gaming terms, what does RPG mean?

A. **Right proper good**

B. **Real player game**

C. **Role playing game**

**12** What's the term given to players and other objects appearing in games?

A. **Splodge**

B. **Spawn**

C. **Spoon**

**13** What do you call the character who searches in Hide and Seek Extreme?

A. **IT**

B. **That**

C. **Leader**

**14** Which of these is not a ROBLOX game genre?

A. **Town and City**

B. **Soccer**

C. **Adventure**

**15** Which game uses a weather machine?

A. **Scuba Diving at Quill Lake**

B. **Booga Booga**

C. **Natural Disaster Survival**

**16** Games which can involve lots of fun little missions and events are often called...

A. **Mini games**

B. **Little LOLs**

C. **Small sports**

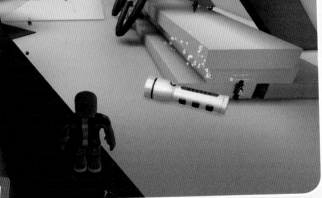

**17** When players instantly reappear in a different location, what is this called?

A. **Telephoning**

B. **Televisioning**

C. **Teleporting**

**18** In the ROBLOX toolbox, what symbol shows that an item is highly recommended?

A. **Orange star**

B. **Orange shield**

C. **Orange fruit**

**19** Who created the popular Jailbreak game?

A. **Dued1**

B. **Badimo**

C. **PrinceHarry**

**20** Do you know what BC is?

A. **Before Computers**

B. **Builders Collaborate**

C. **Builders Club**

## MY QUIZ SCORE:

/ 20

# MY ROBLOX RECORDS!

Fill in your ROBLOX achievements, faves and records...

My ROBLOX name:

I play ROBLOX on: (tick)

PC ☐    Mac ☐    Console ☐    Tablet ☐    Smartphone ☐

My top 5 games:

1.

2.

*TOP GAMES!* →

3.

4.

5.

The first game I played was:

If I created a game it would be called:

My game description would be:

My fave game badges are:

The most Robux I've had is: